Made in United States
North Haven, CT
22 July 2024

55336403R00057